Seasons

WINTER

Belitha Press

Anna Claybourne • Pictures by Stephen Lewis

Belitha Press

First published in the UK in 2001 by
Belitha Press Limited, London House,
Great Eastern Wharf, Parkgate Road,
London SW11 4NQ

Copyright © Belitha Press Limited 2001
Text by Anna Claybourne

ISBN 1 84138 323 6

British Library Cataloguing in Publication Data
for this book is available from the British Library.

Printed in Hong Kong

10 9 8 7 6 5 4 3 2 1

Editor: Veronica Ross
Designer: Kathryn Caulfield
Illustrator: Stephen Lewis
Picture researcher: Juliet Duff
Consultant: Elizabeth Atkinson

Photo Credits
Ancient Art and Architecture Collection: 22, 23.
Bubbles: 26, 29.
FLPA: 16 bottom.
Getty One Stone: 4, 5, 7, 9, 10, 11, 15, 17, 18, 19, 21 both, 24, 25 both.
Robert Harding Picture Library: 8, 16 top.
NHPA: 13, 14.

Every attempt has been made to clear copyrights but should there be
inadvertent omissions please apply to the publisher for rectification.

Contents

Words in **bold** are explained
on pages 30 and 31.

What is winter?

Winter is the darkest, coldest time of the year. The Sun only shines for a few hours each day, and the evenings are long and dark. But winter is also a time for exciting feasts and **festivals**, such as Christmas and New Year.

In winter, you might feel like staying indoors where it's cosy and warm. But going outside can be fun too, especially if it snows. You can make snowmen, go **tobogganing**, and have snowball fights.

Can you see the footprints in the snow in this picture?

Winter Autumn Summer Spring

Winter is one of the four seasons: spring, summer, autumn, and winter. Together the four seasons make up the whole year.

There aren't many animals around in winter. Most of them are hiding from the cold.

winter fact

The fastest winter sport is speed skiing. Skiers can travel at up to 248 kilometres per hour!

Watch out for winter sports, such as skiing, ski jumping, skating and **bobsled** racing. You might even go on a skiing holiday yourself.

How winter happens

Winter always feels colder than the other seasons. This is because in winter, the part of the Earth you live in leans right away from the Sun.

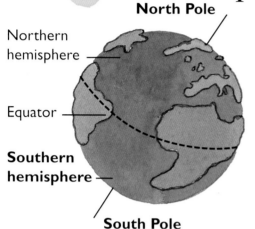

North Pole

Northern hemisphere

Equator

Southern hemisphere

South Pole

The Earth takes a whole year to travel around the Sun. The seasons happen because the Earth is tilted to one side. As it moves, the tilt makes different parts of the Earth face the Sun at different times.

The **equator** divides the Earth into two hemispheres, or halves.

This picture shows the seasons in the **northern hemisphere**.

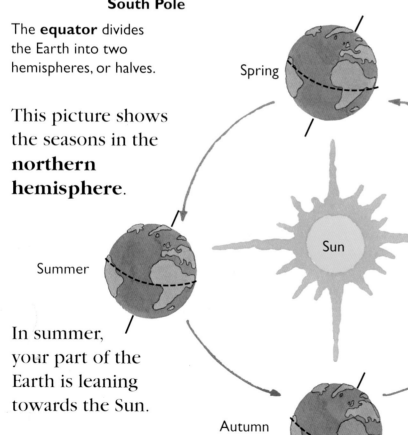

Spring

Sun

Summer

Autumn

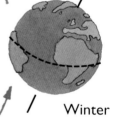

Winter

It is winter when your part of the Earth is leaning away from the Sun.

In summer, your part of the Earth is leaning towards the Sun.

Autumn and spring happen in between winter and summer.

In winter, everyone wears extra-warm clothes to keep the cold out!

If there's lots of snow, you can build a snowman. Use branches for his arms and stones or vegetables for his face. Why not make a snow-woman too?

winter fact

Shadows are longest in winter, because the tilt of the Earth makes the Sun look lower in the sky.

Around the world

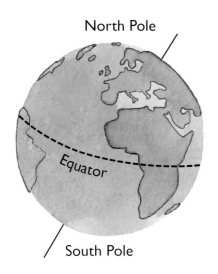

North Pole

Equator

South Pole

The North Pole and the South Pole are the most northern and southern parts of the world.

In North America, Europe and India, winter is in December, January and February. These places are in the northern hemisphere. South America and Australia are in the southern hemisphere. There, winter is in June, July and August.

A cricket match in New Zealand.

In Sweden, the feast of Santa Lucia is held on 13 December. Girls wear white dresses and carry candles in a night-time **procession**.

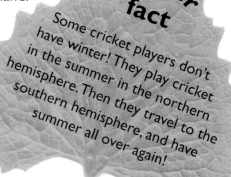

winter fact

Some cricket players don't have winter! They play cricket in the summer in the northern hemisphere. Then they travel to the southern hemisphere, and have summer all over again!

In Scotland, New Year's Eve, on 31 December, is called Hogmanay. People fill the streets to watch huge firework displays.

Fireworks fill the sky on New Year's Eve in Edinburgh, Scotland.

The Chinese New Year festival is in January or February, and lasts for 15 days. People eat special foods such as rice cakes and fortune cookies, and dance in the streets dressed in lion and dragon costumes.

Winter weather

When it's very cold, water turns into ice, or freezes. This means that the **temperature** has dropped below 0 **degrees centigrade**.

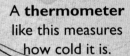

A **thermometer** like this measures how cold it is.

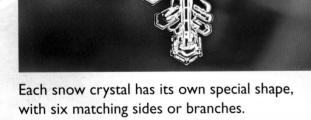

Each snow crystal has its own special shape, with six matching sides or branches.

Snow forms when tiny, invisible drops of water in the air are frozen. They turn into tiny ice **crystals**. As they float around in the sky, the crystals stick together to make fat, fluffy snowflakes.

Only places that are quite far north or south, or very high up, have snow in winter.

In most places near the equator, it's too warm for snow. So there are lots of people in the world who have never seen snowflakes!

When dripping water freezes, **icicles** form. When rain falls on cold surfaces, it can turn into a thick layer of ice.

These oranges have little icicles hanging on them.

In an ice storm, ice forms on rooftops, trees and cables. The ice makes the trees, cables and rooftops very heavy. They sometimes break or snap under the weight.

Plants in winter

In winter, some trees have no leaves at all, while others stay green.

Deciduous trees lose their leaves every autumn. They look very bare during the cold winter months. In spring, they grow new leaves again.

Evergreen trees stay green all winter. They usually have tough, spiny needles instead of leaves.

Evergreen trees often grow on snowy mountains. This is because they are good at staying alive in very cold places.

winter fact

Snowdrops are tiny white flowers that appear at the end of winter. They get their name because they can grow right through the snow!

The holly tree grows red berries in autumn that last through the winter. They make a good snack for hungry birds. But holly berries are poisonous to humans!

Many smaller plants, such as daffodils and nettles, seem to die away in winter. In fact, their roots are still there, under the soil. They are waiting for the spring, when it will be warm enough to grow again.

Animals in winter

In summer, you can see lots of wild animals – frogs, rabbits, birds and butterflies, bees and buzzing flies. So where do they go in winter?

A lot of animals, such as bears, are **hibernating**. That means they've gone to sleep for the winter.

Some insects, such as dragonflies, only fly in summer. In autumn they die, leaving their eggs or babies to survive the winter. Dragonfly babies, called **nymphs**, spend the winter at the bottom of a stream or pond.

Dragonfly nymphs are good hunters. This one has caught another insect to eat.

Frogs sleep in the mud at the bottom of a pond.

winter fact

Fish are still awake in winter, even when they are under thick ice. They swim to the bottom of their river or lake, where it's warmest.

14

Reindeer live in the far north of Russia, Europe and Canada. In winter it is so cold and snowy that they can't find any food. They **migrate** (travel) up to 1000 km southwards in big groups, to find food in the forests.

An arctic fox in her white winter coat.

Some animals, such as mountain hares and Arctic foxes, change colour for the winter.

In summer, mountain hares are brown. In winter, they grow white fur to make them hard to spot in the snow.

When an animal blends in with its background, it is harder for a hunter to see it. This is called **camouflage**.

15

On the farm

Not all crops grow in summer and autumn. For some farmers, winter is a very busy time.

Bees go back to their hives for the winter. They are looked after by beekeepers who feed the bees a mixture of sugar and water to keep them alive.

Honeybees live in hives like this.

In Spain and Morocco, black olives are ready for picking in winter. Everyone joins in to help with the harvest. Then the olives are pressed in a huge olive mill. This squeezes oil out of them. The oil is sold to be used in cooking.

In places such as Scotland and Russia winter can be very cold and snowy. Farm animals have to live indoors in heated sheds.

When the grass is covered in snow, horses, sheep and cows can't eat it. Farmers give them hay (dried grass) or other food instead.

Only the toughest sheep and goats can stay outdoors in the ice and snow.

winter fact

A cat's fur grows longer and thicker in winter to keep it extra warm.

This cat looks fat, but in fact he is fluffing up his thick winter coat to keep out the cold.

17

People in winter

The most important thing to do in winter is to keep warm! People keep warm in lots of ways...

You can wrap yourself up in a winter coat, boots, a hat, a scarf and mittens.

When you feel cold, your body shivers and your teeth chatter. Shivering helps to warm you up.

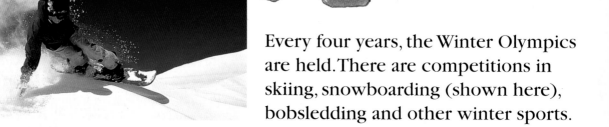

Every four years, the Winter Olympics are held. There are competitions in skiing, snowboarding (shown here), bobsledding and other winter sports.

18

In cold places like Nunavut, in the north of Canada, it's so snowy in winter that people use skis and snowmobiles to get around.

If it's cold at night, you might have to put some extra blankets on your bed.

Heaters and fires keep houses warm and cosy inside. A hot drink helps to warm you up too.

Winter festivals

In many places, Christmas is an important winter festival. It is celebrated on 25 December when **Christians** remember the birth of Jesus Christ. People decorate their houses and give each other presents.

Lots of people who aren't Christians celebrate Christmas too. It's such a big holiday that shops close and trains stop running.

It's a Christmas tradition to kiss under a bunch of mistletoe. This plant grows white berries in winter.

Hannukah is a **Jewish** holiday held for eight days every December. It celebrates a time about 2,200 years ago, when the Jews won a war against the Greeks. At Hannukah, Jewish people eat fried doughnuts, and potato cakes called latkes.

Santa Claus is a magical old man who is said to deliver presents at Christmas.

This Hannukah candlestick, called a menorah, holds nine candles – one for every day of Hannukah, and one to light all the others.

winter fact

People in the southern hemisphere also celebrate Christmas and Hannukah. But their celebrations are in the middle of summer!

These children are at a Christmas party in summer. They live in Mauritius, in the southern hemisphere.

Winter long ago

Hundreds of years ago there were no electric lights. To see on long, dark winter evenings, people used candles, and lamps that burned oil.

If you were very poor and couldn't afford candles or fuel, you would spend most of the winter in the dark!

The Vikings often used sledges to travel across the snow. This is a model of a Viking sledge.

The Vikings lived over 1,000 years ago in cold, snowy places, such as Norway and Iceland. To keep warm in winter, the Vikings covered the insides of their houses with animal furs.

The Vikings believed that their god Woden visited the Earth every winter, from 25 December to 6 January.

The **ancient** Egyptians were the first to have a winter festival, more than 4,000 years ago. When the days started getting longer, they worshipped the Sun for 12 days to welcome it back.

Can you see the rays of the Sun in this ancient Egyptian carving?

At the Roman winter festival, called Saturnalia, children and servants were allowed to run the house.

winter fact

Many ancient peoples celebrated the **winter solstice** – the shortest day of the year. It was a happy time because, when the days started to grow longer, everyone knew spring would come again.

Winter dangers

Ice and snow can be dangerous in winter. You have to be careful not to fall on the slippery ground! If there's ice on the road, cars can skid and crash.

Sometimes rivers and ponds freeze over. It can be very dangerous to walk on them – you might fall through the ice!

This frozen river in Sweden looks very beautiful, but it's not safe to walk on.

Snowploughs push snow off the roads, and trucks scatter grit to make the icy roads less slippery. Some people tie chains around the wheels of their cars to give a better grip.

winter fact

Sometimes ice on roads and pavements is see-through, so it's very difficult to see. It's called black ice and it can cause accidents.

A blizzard happens when thick snow falls on a windy day. The air is so full of snowflakes that you can't see where you are going. It's easy to lose your way and become stuck in the snow.

This car has been buried by a blizzard!

Mountains are very snowy in winter. Wind blows the snow into deep piles.

Sometimes the snow slips. It rushes down the hillside in a huge **avalanche**.

In cold countries, icicles grow every winter. They can hurt you if they fall off and land on you!

These amazing icicles are in Connecticut, USA.

Winter activities

Snow angels

If the snow is quite deep, you can make a snow angel.

Fall on to your back in the snow.
Sweep your arms up and down to make the angel's wings.

Open and close your legs
to make the angel's skirt.

Stand up carefully, turn
around and admire your angel!

Feed the birds

In winter, birds are hungry. You can
feed them by leaving food out on a
windowsill or bird table. They'll love...

- Bits of bacon rind
- Sunflower seeds
- Grated cheese
- Unsalted peanuts
- Coconut pieces

Make decorations

If you're celebrating Christmas, Hannukah, Chinese New Year or another festival, why not decorate your house with paper chains?

Cut coloured or shiny paper into strips about 20cm long and 3cm wide.

Take the first strip and glue or staple it into a ring.

Loop the next strip through the ring and make that into a ring too.

Make a chain by adding more paper rings in the same way.

When it's long enough, pin the chain to a wall, ceiling or window frame.

Winter experiments

Looking at snowflakes

Under a magnifying glass, you can see the amazing shapes snow crystals make. To get a really good look, you'll need:

- A strong magnifying glass
- Some black paper or a piece of black cloth (velvet is best)
- A freezer
- Snow!

Put your black paper or cloth in the freezer to get really cold. When it starts to snow, take the paper or cloth out, go outside and catch some snowflakes on it. Then use the magnifying glass to look at them closely.

Most snowflakes are made out of thousands of tiny crystals clumped together. Gently break up big snowflakes with your finger to separate the crystals. Can you see their six-sided shapes and patterns?

See your breath

If you're outdoors on a very cold day, your breath looks a bit like smoke.

Try making an 'Ooo' sound and blowing a long plume of breath. Can you see it making a cloud in the air?

Then go inside a warm building. Can you still make a breath cloud?

The cloud you can see is made of the tiny drops of water in your breath. They are always there, even when you're indoors.

They are usually too small to see. But very cold air makes them **condense**. This means that they join together and get bigger, so you can see them as a cloud.

Words to remember

ancient
Very old, or a very long time ago.

avalanche
A lot of snow slipping down a mountain.

bobsled
A very fast sledge used in winter sports.

camouflage
Colours or patterns that help an animal blend in with its background.

Christian
A member of the Christian religion. Christians follow the teachings of Jesus Christ.

condense
When water changes from tiny, invisible droplets into bigger water drops which you can see.

crystals
Regular shapes found in ice and many minerals.

deciduous
A tree that loses its leaves in winter.

degrees centigrade
Centigrade is a scale used to measure temperature, or how hot or cold something is. Temperature is measured in units called degrees.

equator
The line around the middle of the Earth. There is no real line there – it only appears on maps and globes.

evergreen
Evergreen trees keep their leaves all year round.

festival
A party or feast to celebrate a special date.

hibernate
To spend the winter asleep. Many animals hibernate.

icicle
A long stick of ice, made by water freezing as it drips off a roof or tree.

Jewish
Jewish people, sometimes called Jews, belong to a very old religion called Judaism. Like Christians and Muslims, Jews believe in one god.

migrate
To travel to another place for part of the year.

northern hemisphere
The northern half of the world, where Europe, America and Russia are.

North Pole
The most northern point on Earth.

nymph
A name for some baby insects.

procession
A parade or walk along a street, as part of a festival.

southern hemisphere
The southern half of the world, where Australia is.

South Pole
The most southern point on Earth.

temperature
How hot or cold something is.

thermometer
A tube full of liquid, used to measure temperature.

tobogganing
Sliding downhill in the snow on a toboggan, sledge or sled.

winter solstice
The shortest day of the year, when your part of the Earth is leaning away from the Sun.

Index